STEP-BY-STEP
CANDLEMAKING

By Mary Carey

Golden Press • New York
Western Publishing Company, Inc.
Racine, Wisconsin

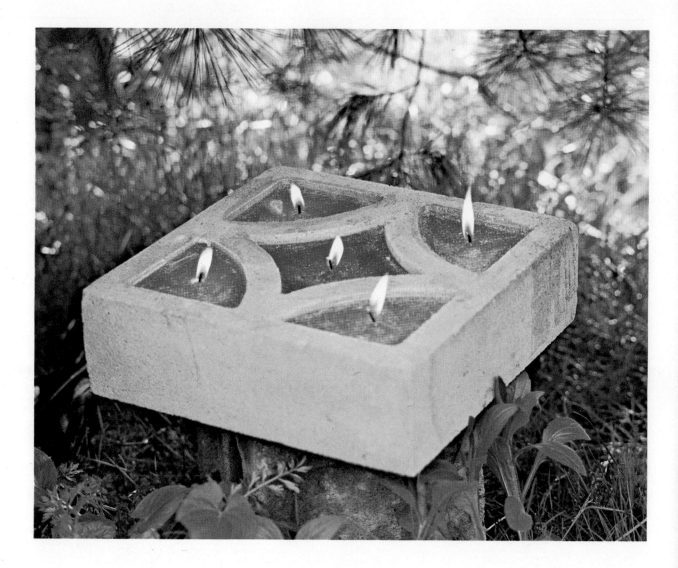

ART DIRECTOR: Remo Cosentino
ART ASSISTANT: Barbara Braunstein
PHOTOGRAPHS: George Ancona
EDITOR: Caroline Greenberg

Contents

Introduction

Who invented candles?

No one knows, and no one ever will know. One might as well ask who first learned to make fire. One might as well demand the name of the genius who invented the wheel.

Long before history began, men rebelled against the tyranny of night and fashioned candles of a sort. These weren't true candles as we know them. They were crude lamps. However, the principle of the oil lamp and the principle of the candle are the same. A wick is suspended in oil. The oil soaks into the wick. When fire is applied to the wick, the oil vaporizes, or turns to gas, and the gas burns with a clear flame.

The true candle—a pillar of wax or a taper with a wick inserted—came into use during the Middle Ages. Then, as now, the finest candles were beeswax. Humble folk did not use beeswax; if they stayed up past sunset they made do with candles of tallow, a fat rendered from beef or mutton.

Tallow candles had their drawbacks, however. They smoked, and they smelled of animal fat. Whenever possible, other substances were used. In the East, a vegetable wax was rendered from berries called candleberries. In the American colonies, the bayberry was popular. Early in the 1700's, spermacet or spermaceti—a white, waxy solid obtained from the head of the sperm whale—became a prized candle material, and after 1850, paraffin became the standard candle material.

Once Mr. Edison invented his incandescent light, candles ceased to be necessities. No one reads or sews by candlelight any more. But candles are still important. We measure a child's progress in life by lighting candles on a birthday cake. At Christmastime, we decorate our homes with candles and we light them as a sign of rejoicing. Candles are lighted in a nine-branched candlestick at Hanukkah, the Jewish Festival of Lights. In many Christian churches, candles burn the year round. The soft, flickering flames are a token of reverence and respect, and the candle may even be considered a symbol of sacrifice, since it consumes itself as it burns.

So candles can be sacred and symbolic. They need not be solemn. They can be simple and beautiful, but they can also be whimsical and charming. We can be serious about them, but there's not really any need for this. Since we don't actually need candles, we can play with them. Candlemaking can be fun and it should be fun. No stunning artistic talent is required. All you need is wax and wick, a kitchen stove, a little time, and the urge to experiment, to express yourself.

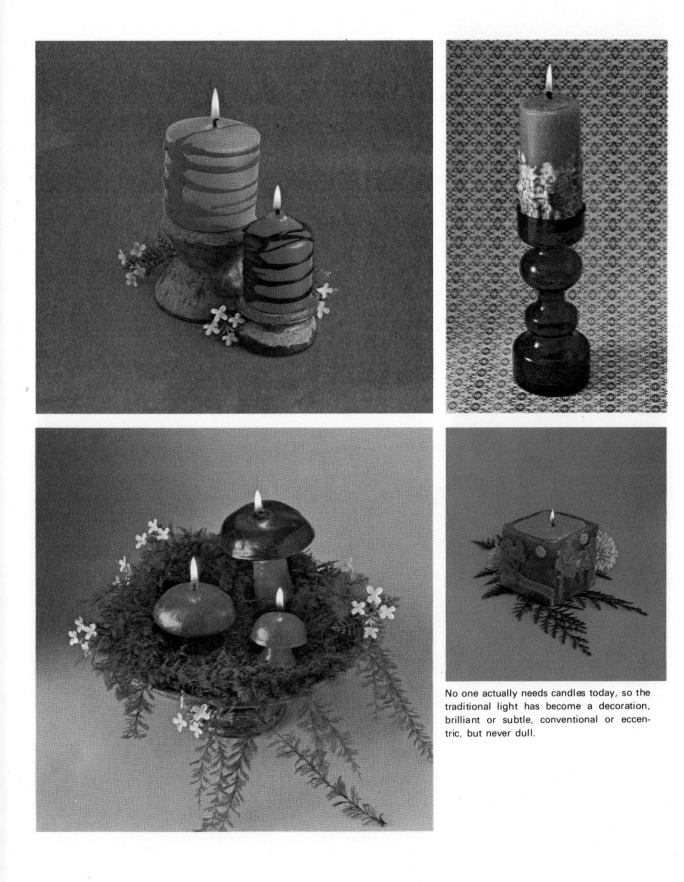

No one actually needs candles today, so the traditional light has become a decoration, brilliant or subtle, conventional or eccentric, but never dull.

Equipment

Strictly speaking, a candle is a piece of wax with a wick embedded in it. Therefore, strictly speaking, one could take a block of paraffin, insert a wick, and call the resulting object a candle. Touch a match to the wick and the thing would burn as candles are supposed to burn. However, even the most undemanding critic wouldn't give a rave review to such a candle, and inserting a wick into paraffin would satisfy no one's creative urge.

If you plan to make candles at all, you owe it to yourself to use the same fine materials that professionals enjoy. Good candlemaking supplies are not very costly, and the results can more than justify the expenditure of a few dollars at your nearby hobby shop.

Wax, Wicking, and Mold

To begin with, provide yourself with a good grade of paraffin and a few yards of wicking. The easiest candle for the novice to make is the poured candle, and for this you will need a mold. Almost anything that can hold melted wax until it hardens can serve as a mold (see pages 30–35), but for the best results you should have at least one finely crafted metal candle mold. These come complete with wick holders, with gaskets or screws for sealing wick holes, and with directions for wicking. If it is cared for properly, a good metal mold will last forever. A one-quart square or round metal mold is most satisfactory for first experiments in candlemaking. (As you gain experience and begin to experiment, you will want to try other kinds of molds and other wicking procedures.)

Stearine

In addition to wax, wick, and mold, you must have stearine. It's a staple with every candlemaker. This substance, derived from fats such as tallow and butterfat, is sold in the form of powdery, white crystals. It is added to melted paraffin to make a finished candle more opaque. Stearine also raises the melting point of paraffin, so that candles do not sag or bend in a warm room. It makes white candles white and colored candles bright.

Dyes

Special candle dyes should always be used for colored candles. These are available in several forms: cakes of intensely colored wax from which small chips can be shaved, granules

Wax, wicking, stearine, mold, mold release, and dyes are basic candle supplies. You also need a melting pot and a candy thermometer. The equipment for cutting wicks, trimming candles, and stirring dyes are probably in your kitchen already. And don't forget newspapers; no one loves a messy candlemaker.

of wax, liquids, and tablets. Don't try to use food coloring, which won't mix with wax, and don't waste time experimenting with crayons. Some crayons contain substances which will cause candles to sputter, and the wax from crayons may not disperse evenly through candle wax.

Mold Release

Nearly every candlecrafter uses a mold release of one type or another. The release is applied to the inside of the mold before the candle is poured, just as butter or margarine is rubbed around the inside of a cake pan before the cake batter is poured. After the candle has hardened in the mold, it will slide out more easily if mold release has been used.

Salad oil makes a fairly satisfactory mold release if it is applied sparingly. Any of the commercial sprays used in cooking will also serve. Hobby shops offer fine silicone sprays especially for candlemaking. When using mold release, it is important not to be too enthusiastic. If you apply too much, droplets may form inside the mold and the finished candle will have little bubbles in the surface. If you use salad oil, wipe the inside of the mold with a tissue before pouring the candle to be sure that you have removed any excess which might mar the candle.

Scents

Scents are not absolutely necessary in a candle, but they are a nice enhancement. Candle scents come in a wide variety, ranging from the familiar bayberry and rose to exotic fragrances like patchouli and frangipani. They are usually oil-based, so that they will blend with wax, and some come complete with directions as to amounts to be added to melted wax. Follow the directions. If you don't have directions, use discretion. A few drops to each pound of wax should be enough. You want a subtle aroma, not a candle that will fairly fumigate a house.

Your supplies for candlecrafting, then, will include wax, wicking, mold, mold release, stearine, dyes, and scents.

Some additional items are required, but these are probably already in your kitchen. Take a quick inventory.

Other Equipment

Do you have a double boiler? You should, since it is safest to melt wax over boiling water. If you don't have a double boiler, you can construct one. Put a trivet in the bottom of a large pan. Pour water into the pan, and then put the pot in which you will melt your wax on the trivet.

You *must* have a candy thermometer. It is necessary to know the temperature of the melted wax at all times, and there is only one way to do this. Clip a candy thermometer to the edge of the melting pot or double boiler and watch the thermometer. If you haven't a candy thermometer, get one. It won't be expensive, and you can't do without it.

You surely already have a water-bath container. This is any vessel, such as a plastic or metal wastepaper basket or a large bucket, which can be partly filled with water. After you have poured hot wax into a mold, you hasten the hardening of the wax by putting the mold into the water bath.

Some molds tend to float when put into a water bath, so keep a heavy object on hand in case you have to weigh the mold down. Nice clean bricks or large trivets make fine weights for molds. Electric irons or large books do not make good weights, since electric irons and books should not be accidentally dropped into water baths.

You can, if you wish, pour wax directly from a double boiler or melting pot into a mold, but it is neater, safer, and more satisfactory to use a container with a handle and a pouring lip. A one-quart Pyrex measuring cup makes a perfect pouring container. A kettle with a pouring spout is also fine, although perhaps not as easy to keep clean.

An ice pick is a great comfort to any candlemaker. Ice picks can be used to chip wax into small chunks for faster melting. As a candle hardens, an ice pick can be inserted into the center to see if the wax has contracted and pulled away from the wick, leaving a cavity that must be filled. An ice pick can also be heated and used as a wick rod to make wick holes in candles which have been molded without wicks. (If you do not have an ice pick, try using a screwdriver—but not too large a screwdriver.)

You will also want a goodly supply of newspapers to spread over your working area, paper towels to wipe things off and clean things up, a paring knife, a pair of kitchen shears for cutting wicking, a hammer for breaking up wax, a tablespoon for measuring stearine, and, since you will be working with hot wax, a pair of pot holders or an oven mitt to protect your hands.

And a stove. Of course you have a stove.

Safety

Wax will burn. It would be of no use in candles if it didn't vaporize and burn. This doesn't mean that candlemakers need constantly dread a wax fire, but it does mean that a little care and the observance of a few rules are required.

Basic Safety Rules

First, melt wax over boiling water. Water cannot get hotter than 212° F. Wax will not vaporize and ignite at this temperature, so the candlemaker who uses a double boiler should not have any difficulties.

Always use a candy thermometer. It isn't necessary to bring wax even to 212° for candlemaking. Watch the thermometer and remove the wax from the heat when it reaches 200°.

Never, never leave melting wax unattended. Even if you are going to step out of the room for only a second, remove the wax from the stove or turn off the burner under the wax.

See to it that the work area where you pour your candles is several steps removed from the stove. You will cover the work area with newspaper to keep wax off counters and tabletops. If the papers are too close to the stove, they may catch fire.

Wax does not bubble and boil, but it does get hot. Use pot holders or oven mitts when handling melting pots or pouring containers, and use only pouring containers with handles and pouring lips or spouts.

When glazing (see page 25), be sure to allow for displacement. For instance, one way to glaze a candle is to dip it into hot water. Be certain the container in which you have heated the water is big enough, and that it is not too full of water. Otherwise, hot water and wax will spill out over the top as the candle is dipped.

Never dip a candle into *boiling* water. Steam rising from boiling water can be hotter than 212° F., and it can also be invisible—super-heated water vapor. Avoid steam burns. Heat water to boiling, then turn off the stove and allow the water to cool for a few moments before dipping your candle.

The candlemaker who uses hot wax for glazing must be even more careful than the one who uses water. Allow plenty of room for the tide of wax to rise in the container when the candle is dipped, and never glaze a candle in a container which has a flame going under it.

It goes without saying that small children and hot wax do not mix. Until a child is old enough, tall enough, and experi-

For safety's sake, be sure the working area where you will pour wax is a few feet away from the stove.

enced enough to handle ordinary cooking chores, he should not be permitted anywhere near a candlemaking operation.

Special Precautions

If you break—or even bend—any of the above rules, be especially wary.

Many candlemakers decide to do a rush job by melting wax directly over the burner. This is not a good idea, since the wax won't heat as evenly. However, if you do decide to melt wax in this manner, don't leave the wax for a moment. Watch the candy thermometer like a hawk. You will find the temperature of wax goes up at an astonishing rate. The instant the thermometer hits 200°, turn off the heat. The wax will then begin to cool, and soon you will have to heat it again. But don't complain. You have to pay for your haste.

Sooner or later, many candlemakers succumb to the temptation to leave wax in the bottom of a melting pot overnight or longer. There is nothing downright sinful about this, but sooner or later the hardened wax will have to be melted again. Naturally, it will melt from the bottom. The liquid wax will then expand and press against the still-solid layer of wax at the top of the melting pot. This pressure should be relieved. Use your ice pick to break through the solid wax, and use it early in the melting process. If you wait too long, liquid wax may spurt up through the solid layer and hit you, the kitchen wall, or the stove.

If wax in the melting pot catches fire, smother the flame with a pot lid. Also, keep an open box of baking soda handy.

In Case of Accident

Prevention is always the best medicine, but even careful candlemakers can have mishaps. There's no real need for trouble, but it's wise to be prepared.

If the wax in your melting pot catches fire, turn off the heat and put a lid on the pot to smother the flames.

Keep an open box of baking soda ready. If wax spills onto the stove it will almost surely burn. Turn off the stove and throw handfuls of baking soda onto the burning wax.

The best protection against a wax fire is a chemical fire extinguisher. These aren't expensive, and most people who indulge in candlecrafting keep one in their work areas.

Never use water to try to put out a wax fire. Water will only splatter the wax, as it would cooking oil, and spread the fire.

If you do have a fire and it seems that things are getting out of control, don't hesitate. Call the fire department.

And if you should spill hot wax on your hands—or any other part of your anatomy—don't try to wipe it off. Run cold water over the wax. It will harden instantly and can be lifted off. Treat the burned area as you would any scald or burn.

If you get hot wax on your hands, don't try to rub it off. Run cold water on the wax; it will harden and lift off.

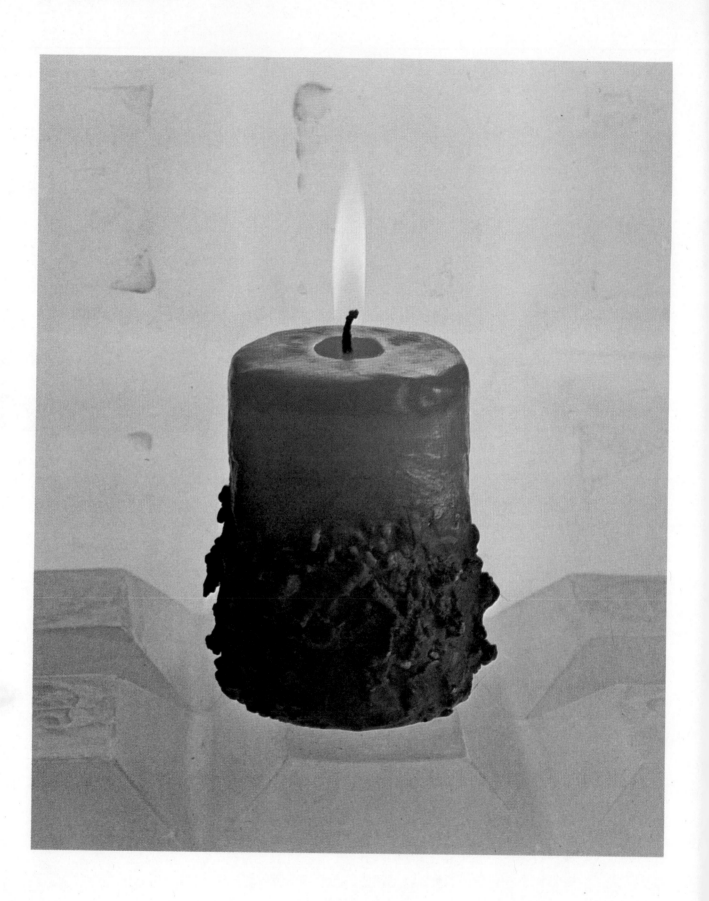

Waxes and Wicks

Undeniably, the finest candle material is still beeswax. It has a high melting temperature, it is fairly pliable even when it's cold, and it produces its own gentle fragrance when it burns. It is, however, so expensive that it is out of the question for the home candlecrafter unless he also happens to keep bees. Today, almost the only place one can see pure beeswax candles is in churches.

This does not mean that beeswax need be completely ignored by the amateur candlemaker. Pre-dyed sheets of beeswax are sold in craft shops and hobby stores, and these can be used to decorate candles. Beeswax is also available in undyed blocks, and some more experienced craftsmen blend beeswax with paraffin to get a scented, long-burning candle. Because beeswax is slightly tacky, it tends to stick to the sides of a mold. If you experiment with beeswax, use mold release and then fill your mold with regular paraffin. Let this set for about ten minutes, then pour out the paraffin that's still liquid. You will have a thin coating of paraffin in the mold; this will prevent the beeswax from sticking and binding the candle to the mold.

Another traditional wax which is still available is bayberry. Like beeswax, it is expensive, since it takes about ten pounds of bayberries to produce one pound of bayberry wax, but few things are nicer for a special gift on a very special occasion than a bayberry candle.

There are special floral or sculpture waxes available in craft shops. These are usually blends of paraffin and beeswax and are intended for use by the craftsman who wants to fashion wax flowers or sculpture decorations for candles. These waxes must be warmed before they are used, but they become pliable and easy to work before they become liquid.

Paraffin Waxes

For all but the most special, precious candles, paraffin wax is completely satisfactory. There are low-temperature paraffin waxes which melt at about 130°, and there are waxes that remain solid until heated to 165° or over, but the most useful and easily obtainable wax is the medium-temperature wax which becomes liquid at about 145°. Some shops carry a medium-temperature wax to which stearine has already been added; this is suitable for most candlemaking. However, for some candles and for glazes, stearine isn't desirable.

The most versatile wax, therefore, is the fine-quality medium-temperature paraffin which is sold in eleven-pound slabs. When it comes from the store it is gray-white and semi-translucent and has a faintly slippery, soapy feeling. The candlemaker can add stearine himself to change the gray-white color to white, and to make this wax more opaque and harder. (The addition of candle dye, of course, will change the color completely.)

Measuring Wax and Stearine

There are no very precise formulas for deciding the proportion of stearine to wax in candles. In a way, candlemaking defies formulas, and most candlemakers have their own ideas about how things should be done. The beginner will want to have some grip on the situation, however, and should assume that for a white candle, at least three tablespoons of stearine should be added to each pound of wax. Dyed candles require only one or two tablespoons per pound. If you miscalculate, you will see why when your candle is unmolded. You have not put in enough stearine if your candle is soapy and too soft. You have put in too much stearine if your candle is brittle and tends to have splintery cracks. You can vary the amount of stearine when the next candle is made.

Add no stearine at all to wax which is used for a glaze.

Cutting chunks of wax from a thick, eleven-pound slab can be a problem, and the solution depends on the temperament and strength of the candlemaker. Some people simply hold the wax in one hand, grasp a hammer in the other, and beat the slab to bits. Some people put the wax slab into a sack or an old pillow case and beat that with a hammer. Some people measure their waxen slabs into precise quarters and delicately chip these away with an ice pick.

Measuring wax and deciding on the amount of stearine to be added can be difficult. If you have a kitchen scale, your problem is solved. If you don't, there are some rules of thumb which can be helpful:

- One eleven-pound slab of wax equals four quarts of liquid wax, more or less.
- If you are using a one-quart mold, hack off about one fourth of the wax from your eleven-pound mold. This will give you from 2¾ to 3 pounds of wax.
- Remember that you will never come out even to the last decimal point. Don't let this worry you. An ounce or two one way or another will not make any difference.
- Also remember that after you have molded your candle, you will have wax left over. This is not a problem. Save the wax for your next candlemaking session; it won't spoil.

Most paraffin comes in eleven-pound slabs. Other sizes are also available, and some are scored, as shown above. The size of the wicking you select depends on the size of your mold.

Wicks

Choosing the proper wick can be even trickier than measuring wax. Here, experimentation really comes in, and you will not know how successful you have been until you light your finished candle.

For most candles which are poured into regular candle molds, a plain braided wick is used. The size of the wick depends on the size of the mold. For candles two inches in diameter or smaller, use a small wick. A medium square-braid wick is suitable for candles from two to four inches in diameter, and any wax pillar candle bigger than four inches requires a larger wick. Trial and error is the best way to decide which wick to use with which mold. The mold manufacturers attempt to make it as easy as possible for their customers. Each commercial mold comes complete with a length of wicking which should be the right size for the mold. Try to match this size wick for future castings in the mold.

Wire-core Wicks

Some candles are molded without wicks, and the wick is added after the candle has hardened (see stack candles, for example, on page 40). For this type of candlemaking, a metal-core wick is indispensable. Like the regular braided wick, the metal-core wick is made of cotton yarn, and it comes in several sizes. In the center of each of these wicks is a fine wire—magnesium, lead, or steel. This wire, which makes the wick fairly rigid, is so slender that it will vaporize and burn when the candle is lighted. To use the wire-core wick, the candlemaker heats an ice pick and applies it to the finished candle to make a wick hole. He then inserts the metal-core wick into the hole (see photograph) and seals the hole with a small amount of warm wax.

Wire-core wicks are slightly rigid, and can be added to a candle after it is unmolded. Make a hole in the candle with a hot ice pick, dip the wick into warm wax, pull it taut, and then insert it into the wick hole.

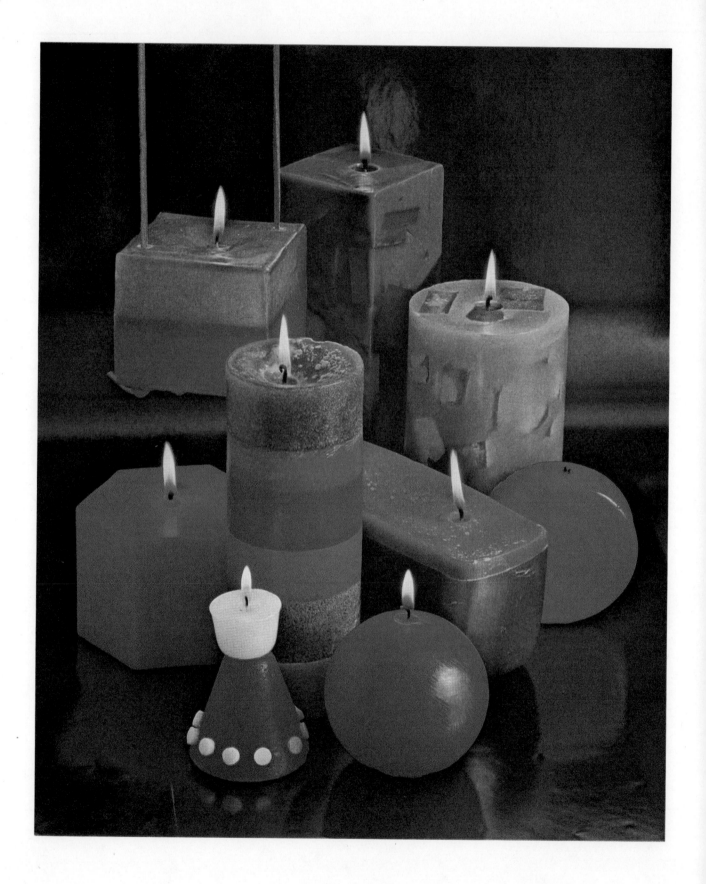

Color

Candle dyes are pure pigment suspended either in wax or in oil. They are so concentrated that a red dye can appear almost black and a bright yellow may look like a very deep brown.

Unless you plan to go into candlemaking on a truly enormous scale, do not attempt to bypass the craft shops and mix your own dyes. The pigment is a fine powder, and the slightest draft will set it swirling through the air. Even professionals have had their troubles with pigments, and only a mother can love a bright blue candlecrafter.

Use the dyes which are sold especially for candles. The range of colors available is enormous. You can purchase deep red, hot pink, orange, yellow, lavender, purple, bright blue, brown, black, and almost any shade in between.

Mixing Colors

If you wish, you can start out with the three primary colors: red, yellow, and blue. Remember the art classes you had in elementary school and blend your own shades. For example:

Pink is red plus white, so for a pink candle add only a tiny amount of red dye to your candle wax and increase the amount of stearine you use.

The novice candlemaker can start with as few as three colors. Just remember the color wheel (above): combine yellow and blue to get green; blue and red for purple; and red mixed with yellow for orange. You can vary the intensity of color in dyed wax by using greater or lesser amounts of dye (left).

There is a certain amount ot guesswork in all candlemaking. What color will the finished candle be when it is unmolded? You can get some idea by dropping a bit of wax into a cup of cold water. As the wax hardens, you can tell approximately how intense the color will be in the finished candle.

Orange is red plus yellow.

Blue and yellow will give you green—light green or dark green, depending on the proportion of yellow to blue.

Red and blue equals purple.

Green and red produce brown.

If you find the dyes too brilliant and you wish to mute the color of your finished candle, add a bit of black.

Adventure with color all you please. Mix and blend to your heart's content. But don't be hasty when putting dye into melted wax. The dye is extremely strong, and a tiny bit at a time should be added. It is easy to put dye into wax, but it's impossible to get it out again once it's there, so proceed with care.

Testing for Color

The color of the melted wax in the double boiler or melting pot will not be the true color of the finished candle. As the wax sets up in the mold and becomes solid and opaque, the dye color will become deeper and richer. Some experts recommend testing color by dropping a spoonful of dyed wax onto a white surface—a saucer, perhaps, or the top of the refrigerator. When the wax hardens, the color will be a shade or two lighter than it will appear in the finished candle, since not that much wax is involved. However, this method will give you an approximate idea of the color your candle will be.

An alternate testing method—and one which will relieve you of the chore of scraping wax off the saucer or the refrigerator—is to drop a spoonful of wax into a cup of cold water. The wax will harden immediately, and you can see the true color you will obtain. But again, this small bit of hardened wax will probably be lighter than the entire finished candle.

Casting a Candle: Basic Steps

Before you begin, assemble your supplies and prepare your work area. The work area is the area where you will pour wax into the mold, put the mold in the water bath, and, later, unmold the candle. For safety's sake, this area should be a few feet removed from the stove.

Cover the area—counter or tabletop—with newspapers. Also, spread newspapers on the floor in front of the work area to catch any stray wax which may spill in the candlemaking process. (No matter how careful you are, there's probably going to be *some* spilled wax.)

Check your supplies against the following list. You should have:

Wax	**Weight** for holding the mold down in the water bath
Wicking	
Mold	**Pouring container,** such as a Pyrex cup. It must have a handle and a pouring lip.
Stearine	
Dyes	
Mold release	
Scents	**Wick rod** (ice pick or screwdriver)
Double boiler or melting pot and pan	
	Paper towels and newspapers
Candy thermometer	
Water-bath container	**Pot holders or oven mitts**

In addition, you will want a **hammer,** to help break chunks of wax from your eleven-pound slab, a **paring knife,** if you are using a dye which comes in the form of a solid cube of wax, **scissors** for cutting wicking, and an old **tablespoon** for measuring stearine, mixing in dyes, and ladling out dyed wax for the color test.

Don't forget to open a box of baking soda.

Melting the Wax

The first step in candlemaking is to break a suitable amount of wax from the eleven-pound slab. Break the wax into small chunks for quicker melting.

Put water in the bottom of your double boiler, put wax chunks in the top and place over the heat. As the wax begins to melt, slip the candy thermometer onto the edge of the double boiler or the melting pot so you can keep track of the temperature of the wax at all times.

Wax should always be melted over boiling water, and the ideal melting pot is a double boiler. Break wax into small chunks for quicker melting.

While wax is melting, prepare mold. First, spray it with a mold release or coat it with salad oil.

Next, insert wick into mold. This commercial metal mold is sealed at the bottom with a rubber gasket.

Fasten the wick to the wick holder. Be sure wick is in the center of the mold or your candle will burn unevenly.

While you are wicking your mold, keep an eye on the candy thermometer in your melting wax.

When wax is at 180°—190°, add stearine—three tablespoons to a pound of wax for a white candle, less for a dyed one.

Add dye, a tiny bit at a time. Test for finished color by dropping a spoonful of wax into a cup of water.

Turn off the burner or remove the melting pot from the stove, then add scent just before pouring candle.

Before putting melted wax into a pouring container, wipe melting pot to keep drops of water out of the wax.

Use an oven mit when pouring warm wax into a mold; tilt the mold to keep air bubbles from forming in your candle.

Once you have started melting wax, do not leave the kitchen. Check the candy thermometer often, and also make sure that the water under the melting pot or in the bottom of the double boiler has not boiled away.

Preparing the Mold—and Wicking

While the wax is melting, prepare the mold.

First, spray the inside of the mold with a commercial release or coat it with salad oil. Make sure that you don't overuse the release. A very thin coat is adequate.

Next, insert a wick into the mold. All commercial molds come with instructions for wicking, and these should be read carefully. The wicking process, however, is usually the same for all molds:

Cut a piece of wicking which is several inches longer than the mold.

If you have a mold which has come with a retainer disc (a rubber gasket), thread the wick through the hole in the bottom of the mold and make a knot in the wick below the hole. Slide the retainer disc onto the wick between the knot and the hole and pull the wick up through the mold until the retainer disc and the knot are held firmly against the bottom of the mold. Place the wick holder across the top of the mold and secure the wick to this.

The wick should be positioned so that it is in the center of the mold. It should not sag or bend, but it should not be pulled too tight or the retainer disc may spread, letting melted wax escape through the bottom of the mold.

If your mold has a retainer screw for sealing the bottom, you will find it easier to thread the wick through the wick hole; pull it up through the mold and fasten it to the wick holder. Then draw the wick until it is tight, but not too tight, insert the retainer screw into the wick hole, wind the wick around the retainer screw, and tighten the screw with a screwdriver.

Mold sealer—a puttylike substance—is often recommended for sealing the bottoms of molds which have retainer screws. Masking tape can also be used.

For a fine, even finish on a candle, it is wise to pour melted wax into a warm mold. Heat metal molds by putting them into a warm oven for a few minutes. The key word is "warm." The oven should not be hot. Turn it to the lowest temperature, put the mold on the grid well away from the floor of the oven, and leave the oven door open. Fine metal molds are put together with solder, and you don't want to melt the solder and ruin the mold. Also, you don't want to

Use mold sealer (a puttylike substance) or masking tape to seal the bottoms of molds that have retainer screws.

A fine glaze can be obtained by dipping a candle into hot wax. The eggshell candles shown below were molded of white wax. Adding a glaze of colored wax gives a beautiful, translucent Easter-egg effect.

When glazing a candle, remember to use plenty of extra wick (the best and safest way to dip a candle is by the wick). Also, allow for displacement: the level of hot wax in the glazing container will rise as the candle is lowered into it. As the amateur candlemaker becomes more proficient and strives for special finishes on his candles, he may decide to fashion a special glazing container. These are usually several inches in diameter, but quite deep—a foot and a half or more—so the candlemaker can dip his candle without fear of hot wax running out over the top.

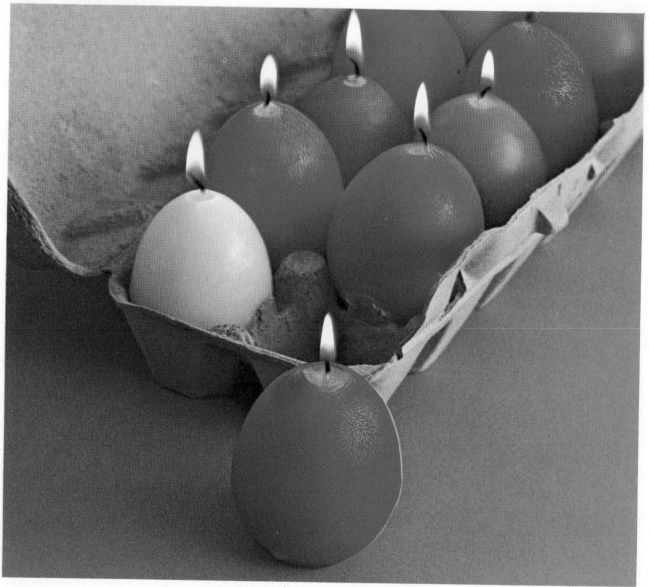

heat the mold to the point where it will be difficult to handle.

Now put cool—not cold—water in the water-bath container.

While you have been preparing the mold, you have also been watching the candy thermometer. When the wax reaches a temperature of about 180° to 190°, add stearine—three tablespoons to a pound of wax for a white candle, and one or two tablespoons for a colored one.

Stir in the stearine and add dye, a tiny bit at a time.

When the dye is completely dispersed through the melted wax, test for color either by dropping the wax onto a white surface or by putting some wax into a cup of water.

When your wax reaches 200°, remove it from the heat immediately.

Pouring

You are now ready to pour the candle. (If you are going to add scent, now is the time; follow the directions on the bottle.)

Pouring will be done in the work area, away from the stove.

It is important that not a single drop of water gets into the wax, so remove any condensed moisture from the bottom of the melting pot or double boiler with paper towels.

If the melting pot has a pouring lip or spout, pour directly from the pot into the warm metal mold. If the melting pot does not have a pouring lip, use a pouring container which does—and the one-quart Pyrex measuring cup, with its wide top, is perfect for this purpose. (To prevent the wax from cooling too quickly in the cup, you can warm the cup in the oven at the same time you warm the mold. Then pour the melted wax from the melting pot into the Pyrex cup.)

Reserve a small amount of wax in the melting pot—a half to one cup will be sufficient—and put the melting pot back onto the heated water.

Use oven mitts or pot holders to hold the warm mold and the pouring container.

Tilt the mold slightly and pour melted wax down the side of the mold to prevent air bubbles from forming. Fill the mold to within an inch or two of the top, or until you have a candle as tall or short as you desire—considering the size of the mold, of course.

Pouring Temperature

Wax poured into a metal mold should be about 180° to 190°. It should never be hotter than 200°. If you pour the wax when it is too hot, you may pit the surface of the candle with steam bubbles. If you let the wax get too cold before pouring, you may have air bubbles in the candle.

The Water Bath

After pouring the wax into the mold, set the mold in the water bath to harden. The water in the water-bath container should be deep enough so that it reaches almost to the top of the mold, but not so deep that water will run over into the mold. If you have miscalculated and the water in the container is not quite deep enough, don't attempt to add more after the mold is in the container. You don't want to get water into the mold, and you don't want little wavy lines in the finished candle—and either of these things may happen if you try to add water after the mold is in the bath.

Weigh the mold down if necessary.

Filling "Well Areas"

After the candle has cooled in the water bath for about half an hour, reheat the wax you have reserved in the melting pot.

You will see that a scum has formed on top of the candle. Insert an ice pick into the candle next to the wick two or three times to break this scum and relieve the surface tension of the wax. A cavity in the candle, called a well area, will be apparent. This is caused by the contraction of the wax as it cools. Fill this cavity with the wax you have reserved. Use the pyrex cup or the pouring container with lip or spout to fill the well area. Don't add so much wax that it rises beyond the first pouring, or the wax may seep down between the mold and the candle, ruining the surface of the candle.

Wait another half an hour and again use the ice pick to test for cavities. If any appear, refill the well areas.

In another half hour, test again for cavities and refill any well areas.

After two to three hours, remove the mold from the water bath. Let the candle continue to cool inside the mold for another six to eight hours. It should be completely cold to the touch before you attempt to unmold the candle. Most candlemakers let pillar candles cool overnight and then unmold them.

Unmolding

Unmolding should be simple if you have used a mold release. Undo the gasket and knot at the bottom of the mold, or remove the masking tape and unscrew the retaining screw. Remove the wick holder. Turn the mold upside down and tap it gently on a surface which is covered with some padding (such as a folded towel or a piece of old sheeting folded several times). The candle should slide out easily.

If the candle does not release from the mold immediately, don't try to force it by hammering on the mold. You will only

The water in the water bath should be cool but not cold, and deep enough so that it reaches to the level of the wax.

After candle has cooled in the bath, break the surface tension with an ice pick and fill cavities with warm wax.

damage the mold. Instead, put the mold into the refrigerator for fifteen or twenty minutes and chill it slightly. (Don't use the freezer. Candles which have been chilled too severely in refrigerators or in ice-cold water baths may develop unsightly cracks called thermal fractures.)

When the candle is chilled, again tap the mold on the padded surface. The candle should be released.

If no amount of persuasion succeeds in getting the candle out of the mold, you can release it by pouring hot water over the mold. The wax adhering to the walls of the mold will melt slightly and the candle will slide out. The candle will not have a fine, smooth surface, but you will have saved the mold for future use and you can always melt the damaged candle down and try again.

Since most molds have seams, your candle will probably have one of more seam lines on it. Remove these by sliding a paring knife along the lines. A feather touch is required for this operation, since you don't want to gouge the candle.

Glazing

Candles poured in good metal molds usually don't require glazing, but if you wish to glaze a candle, do it at this point, before trimming off the extra wick. Holding the candle by the wick, dip it quickly into either hot water or hot wax. (See page 22.)

A reminder: Wax used for glazing should not contain stearine, since a glaze should be translucent. Also, make sure there is room in the container for the water or wax to rise as the candle is dipped.

Finishing

After glazing, let the surface of the candle get completely cold and hard.

Finish the candle by trimming the extra wick from top and bottom. It is unlikely that the bottom of the candle will be absolutely even. Correct this by using a cheese grater to trim off excess wax, then smoothing the bottom of the candle by rubbing it gently on a heated skillet.

If the surface of the candle has been marred by handling, rub away the imperfections with an old nylon stocking.

Use mold release so that your candle will slide out of the mold easily. Don't try to force it by banging the mold.

If the finished candle has a seam line from the mold, you can gently smooth it away with a paring knife.

A Candle Is for Burning

Candles are more beautiful when they are burning. People look better by candlelight, too. Don't try to save the candles you have made. Unless you want to give them as gifts, use them and enjoy them. Touch a match to the wick and see what happens.

If you have figured correctly on the relative size of mold and wick, there will be a lovely glow and a minimum of dripping. If you have made a miscalculation, it will show up when the candle is burned.

If your candle flame burns down immediately into the candle, is drowned in melted wax and goes out, your wick is too small. You can make a note of this, and use a slightly larger wick the next time you cast a candle in that particular mold.

If the flame flares up and melts out the sides of the candle, the wick is too large. Use a smaller one next time.

If the wick burns part way down the candle, then suddenly blazes, drops over, and burns through the wall of the candle, causing hot wax to cascade out, you probably have an air pocket inside the candle. Next time, be more careful when filling well areas.

Do not be distressed if any of these things happen when you light your finished candle. You will learn from your small mistakes, and small mistakes in wax are not large disasters. If you can't tolerate a drooping or drowning candle, break it up, retrieve the wick, melt down the wax, and begin again.

One candle which will sooner or later drown its own flame is the large-diameter wax pillar. A candle which is three, four, or five inches in diameter will not consume itself entirely even when a large wick is used. Instead, the wick burns down, causing a cavity in the center of the candle, and the outer walls of the candle remain solid.

If the large-diameter candle is especially lovely and you want to keep it forever, you can. After the wick has burned down an inch or two below the top of the candle, blow out the flame. Scoop out extra wax before it has a chance to harden. Into the resulting cavity, insert a votive light in a glass container. Light the votive light, burn it until it is consumed, then replace it with another votive light. You can keep your large candle as long as you like and burn it as often as you please.

Since there are few set rules about candles, there is no set rule that large-diameter candles must be preserved like family heirlooms. You can disregard the votive lights and use the big candle as a glow candle. When the wick has burned down an inch or two—and threatens to expire in a small sea of wax—blow out the flame. Use a steel spoon to remove the soft, warm wax from around the wick. Do this with care, so as not to break off the wick. Then relight the candle. The flame will glow softly through the wax walls of the candle.

If you follow this routine, you will eventually have a deep well in the large-diameter candle. Use a long match—one of those made especially for lighting fires in fireplaces—to light the candle without burning your fingers.

Whatever you do, never drop match stubs onto the top of a candle. The paper stubs will soak up wax and become extra wicks—giving much more flame and much more muss than you need or want.

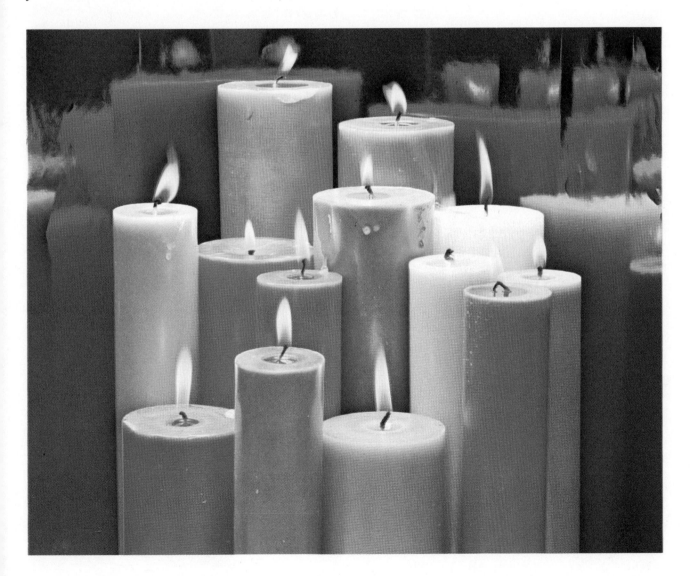

Helpful Hints

Candlemaking is a creative occupation, and like many creative occupations, it can be messy. The candlemaker is apt to have wax on his shoes, just as the painter is apt to have daubs of color on his shirts. The candlecrafter will wear old shoes, therefore, as well as old clothes. But unlike the painter or the sculptor, the candlemaker does not often work in a special studio. He works in a kitchen, and it behooves him to tidy up after he finishes work.

The first rule to remember when cleaning up after making candles is: *Never pour wax down a drain.* Woe to the craftsman who ignores this warning. The wax will harden immediately in the pipes and the plumber will have to be summoned.

Leftover Wax

There will be wax left over; there is *always* wax left over. Heat this in the melting pot, then pour it into a cake pan which has been coated with mold release. When it has hardened in the pan, turn it out, break it into chunks, and put it away to use another day. To prevent it from getting dusty, wrap it in plastic, or store it in a jar with a good lid.

If part of your original slab of wax remains intact, wrap that in plastic, too, before putting it away.

If you have used hot water to glaze a candle, let the water get cold. Some wax will have melted and mixed with the water. When the water is cold, this wax will rise to the top and solidify. It can be lifted off, broken up, and stored away.

Cleaning Your Equipment

Clean the melting pot or double boiler, your ice pick, and all other utensils by heating them in a warm oven. Set the oven at low, cover a shelf with aluminum foil to catch any wax drippings, and let the wax melt off the utensils onto the foil.

When the utensils are warm and apparently wax free, wipe them with a paper towel. Then wash them with hot water.

Purists and demon housekeepers clean their molds after finishing their candles. The process is the same as for utensils and melting pots. Turn the molds upside down and put them into a warm—not hot—oven on a sheet of aluminum foil. Leave the oven door open so the molds don't get too hot and the solder doesn't melt.

After the wax has dripped off the molds, wipe out the molds with a soft cloth, spray them with mold release to prevent rust, wrap them in plastic, and put them away.

Pour leftover wax into a cake pan. When it is hard, turn it out, break it into chunks, and either wrap it in plastic or put it into a jar to keep it clean.

Clean molds and utensils by putting them on a sheet of aluminum foil in a warm oven. The wax will melt off onto the foil. Leave the oven open to prevent overheating, smoke, or a possible wax fire.

Scouring material should never be used on a fine metal mold. The inside of the mold must be unscratched so that candles will release easily. The experienced candlemaker will not even prod at the inside of a mold with a fingernail.

Mold holders, retaining screws, and rubber gaskets can be stored inside the molds, but they should be wrapped in plastic so they don't scratch the mold.

Some candlemakers who are not purists don't clean their molds at the end of the candlemaking operation. They announce—and with some justification—that enough mold release and wax remain on the molds to prevent rusting. They simply wrap the molds in plastic to keep the dust off and store them away.

Whether you store the molds shining clean or daubed with wax, see that they are protected from dust.

Don't forget to remove the aluminum foil from the oven when you have finished cleaning your utensils. After the oven has cooled, examine it to make sure no drops of wax have gotten onto the oven floor or the walls.

Fold up the newspapers you have used in your work area and throw them away. Keeping wax-spattered paper is not a good idea because it is inflammable.

If you have gotten wax onto any item of clothing, remove the hardened wax with a table knife. Then either wash the clothing or send it to the cleaner—explaining to the cleaner the sort of spot he has to deal with. The spot should come out.

Molds

The novice candlecrafter who starts out with one metal mold usually adds to his stock before long. The mold-makers offer a marvelous variety. There are tall molds and short ones. Some are square and some are round and some are oval. There are hexagonal molds and star-shaped molds, molds for squat candles and molds for towering, tapered pillars of wax. And there are two- and three-part molds in metal and in plastic (see page 34).

The professionally crafted mold is beautiful in itself. The candles cast in it are beautiful. But there is no reason why a candlemaker need confine himself to this sort of mold. Almost anything with a cavity in it can be a mold, and candlemaking is an endless experiment, anyway. So don't be inhibited. Experiment to your heart's content.

Molds Around the Home

How many molds do you have? Look around your house. You may be surprised.

Do you have a metal mold for fancy gelatin desserts? Then you also have a metal mold for fancy candles.

A muffin tin is handy for stack candles (see page 40).

Small aspic molds (the ones designed to mold individual servings of aspic) are good if you want to make **"floaters"**—small candles which can be floated in water as part of a flower arrangement. The contours of the aspic molds are more interesting than those of plain baking containers like muffin tins, and putting a wick into a floater is the easiest thing in the world. Use a small wire-core wick (see page 15) and insert it into the aspic mold as the wax begins to harden in the mold. Hold the wick steady for a minute or two until the wax starts to scum. (Be sure the wick is in the center of the mold, or your floater will burn unevenly and tilt to starboard.)

Pyrex baking dishes and custard cups can be first-class molds. They are heat-resistant and inexpensive, and they come in a number of sizes.

Ordinary glassware (not fine crystal, unless you don't mind risking it) can also be used to mold candles. For a pleasing, cone-shaped candle, try pouring wax into a pilsner glass. Juice glasses are good for small candles, and highball glasses will do for tall candles. The possibilities are endless. Open your cupboard doors and see what you have.

Bear one thing in mind when selecting molds from your cupboard. You want to get your candle out of the highball

Small aspic molds are perfect for making candles which can be floated in water, either all by themselves or as part of a flower arrangement.

Muffin tins and aspic molds take to hot wax readily. Glassware and plastic require more care. Pour into glass at about 170°; if you use plastic, let your wax cool until a scum forms on top of it.

glass—or the aspic mold—or the custard cup—once the wax has hardened. Containers which are wider at the top than at the bottom, such as pilsner glasses and aspic molds, are easier when it comes to unmolding. Containers with straight sides can be used, however. Coat the container with mold release before pouring wax. If the candle doesn't release after it has hardened, you need not give up and throw away the glass. Put it into hot water until the wax has softened, then turn the container upside down and let the wax slide out. Clean the glass as you would clean any candlemaking utensil—by putting it into a warm (not hot) oven, and then washing it.

Wicking After Unmolding

Except for floaters, you will probably mold candles in muffin tins, glasses, and Pyrex dishes without wicks. Wicks can be inserted after a candle is unmolded. Use a wire-core wick. Dip it into warm wax and pull it taut. Then, with a heated ice pick, make a wick hole in your candle. Insert the wire-core wick into this hole (see picture on page 15) and seal the hole by pouring a tiny bit of warm wax around the wick.

Well Areas

Cooling wax contracts and forms well areas in regular candle molds. Cooling wax will also contract in a muffin tin or a

If you want to use a glass container as a candle holder (see page 61), you should pre-wick the glass. Tie a wire-core wick to a wick holder and suspend the wick in the glass before filling it with wax. (You risk shattering the glass if you use a hot ice pick to make a wick hole after wax has hardened.)

highball glass. The fact that you are molding a candle without wicking will not make the slightest difference—you will still have a depression in the center of the wax. Reserve some melted wax, as you would if using a regular mold, and use it to fill this depression so that the top of the candle will be even.

Pouring Temperatures for Metal and Glass Molds

Pouring temperatures for metal containers should be the same as for professional metal molds—180° to 200°. If you use glass, let the wax cool at least to 170° before pouring, and warm the glass first by putting it into the oven and setting the heat at low—very low. Leave the oven door open so that the glass doesn't overheat and shatter.

Disposable Molds

Though food packagers aren't often accused of thinking over-much about wax, many containers for food and drink make odd and interesting candle molds.

Little tubs for soft margarine can become little tubs of wax—once the margarine is consumed. Turn the hardened wax out of the margarine tub, add a wick (see page 15), and you have a chunky little candle.

Cardboard milk cartons have been with us for some time. If you have worked with a good square metal mold, a milk carton may seem clumsy, but don't overlook it entirely. Milk cartons do work fairly well, and if you want to mass-produce square candles, milk cartons can be handy indeed—and they can be disposed of without a qualm.

Don't throw away your empty beer or soft-drink cans. They make very satisfactory molds. Or check your stock of canned vegetables and juices. Vegetable and juice cans come in all sizes, from tiny to jumbo.

An empty cottage cheese container can be a candle mold, and so can an empty ice-cream carton.

Food containers aren't the only molds the grocer provides. Even the cardboard core from a roll of paper towels offers possibilities. Seal one end with a cardboard disc held in place with masking tape and you have a mold for a tall, slender candle. Coat the inside with release. (You won't be able to spray the inside of this mold, but you can pour in salad oil, swish it around, and then pour off the excess.) You will have to destroy the cardboard cylinder to get the candle out, but that's no problem. There will be another cardboard cylinder available as soon as you've used the next roll of paper towels.

This candle is made of brown wax topped with white whipped wax which has been dribbled down the side for a realistic beerstein effect. (See pages 59–60 for directions on whipping wax.) The glass was wicked before the wax was poured, as shown on page 31.

Almost anything that will hold food can be a candle mold. Straight-sided containers and those with wide tops can be re-used. The unusual layered candle above was made in a cardboard carton which was cut away when the candle was unmolded.

Cottage cheese cartons and beer or soft-drink cans can be used again and again. If the container is wider at the top than at the bottom, or if it has straight sides, the candle should release without difficulty. Always use mold release, and if there is an indentation at the top of a can which might bind the candle and prevent it from sliding out, remove this with a pair of metal cutters. However, don't try to use coffee cans to mold candles. Nearly all coffee cans have indentations running around the sides, and there's just no way to get a candle out.

Unmolding Narrow-neck Molds

If you greatly admire the shape of a plastic or glass container which has a narrow neck, you can use it as a mold if you don't mind destroying it when you release your candle. You might happen across a well-designed pickle bottle or an elegant jar of mustard, or perhaps some handsomely packaged instant coffee. After eating the pickles or using the mustard or drinking the coffee, clean the container well. If it's glass, warm it as you would any glass mold. Fill it with wax. The wax will contract and you will have to refill well cavities.

When the wax is completely hard, break the glass container. Wrap it in a piece of sheeting or in several layers of paper towels so that bits and pieces of glass can't fly around the kitchen. Then tap it gently with a hammer.

The Christmas-tree candle above was made in the two-part plastic mold shown. Commercial molds like this one come with complete instructions, plus wicking, and make it possible for the candlecrafter to turn out candles in many shapes.

The candles on the right were all molded in ordinary household containers. Two mixing bowls were used to form the yellow candle on the right, and a glass tumbler and a paper cup were used for the other two. The unusual candle with découpage decoration in the picture above right was poured in a canned ham tin. Directions for joining and wicking stacked candles are given on pages 40–42.

Unmolding Plastic Containers

Plastic won't break as glass does, and plastic bottles and jars can offer problems when used as candle molds. The procedure for molding is the same as that for molding in glass bottles, but unmolding is something else. The plastic will have to be cut away from the candle with a sharp knife or a razor blade. Test the top edge of the container to see how easily it will cut. If you have encountered an especially tough piece of plastic, you may decide against attempting to mold a candle in that particular container.

Wicking Cardboard Molds

When using food containers as molds, it is often easier to pour the candle and let it harden, then unmold it and add a wire-core wick (see page 15). Cardboard containers can be wicked, however. With an ice pick, make a small hole in the bottom of the container. Thread the wick through and tie a knot in it below the hole. Seal the wick hole with mold sealer or masking tape. Fasten the top of the wick to a wick holder. (This need not be a special object made only to hold wicks. A lollipop stick or a pencil will do. Tie the wick to the stick or pencil, or tape the wick to the holder with masking tape.)

Many hobby shops offer wick clips—little pieces of metal which are helpful in wicking a cardboard mold. They prevent the wick from breaking through into the mold.

Use a light touch when wicking cardboard. If you pull the wick too taut, you may pull out the bottom of the container, or crumple the top.

Pouring Temperatures for Cardboard and Plastic Molds

When using cardboard molds, let the melted wax cool almost to 145°—or until it has a scum on the top—before you pour. If the wax is too hot, it may burst through the container.

Plastic containers can be slightly more heat-resistant than cardboard, but don't count on it. Cool the melted wax at least to 150° before pouring into plastic. Pour a small bit at first, to see how well the plastic stands up. If it holds its shape, fine. Go ahead and fill the container. If it doesn't hold its shape, you are out nothing but one disposable container, and you haven't spilled hot wax all over the kitchen counter.

Cardboard containers can be wicked before a candle is poured, and so can tin cans. Use an ice pick to make a hole in the bottom. Thread the wick through the hole and fasten it to a wick holder laid across the top of the container. Seal the hole in the bottom with masking tape.

Layered Candles

Leftover wax is no embarrassment. Candlemakers *always* have some wax left over, and there's no need to let this wax go to waste. Let it get hard, then break it into chunks and wrap the chunks in plastic so that they stay clean. You can remelt the wax and use it anytime you want to.

Making a layered candle is one way to use leftover wax. Two different colors of wax are adequate for a layered candle. Three colors are more fun, and you can use as many as four or five. Suit yourself about color combinations. A layered candle can be as muted or as mad as you please.

You must have more than one pouring container for a layered candle, since you must keep several batches of dyed wax molten at the same time. The pouring containers must have handles and pouring lips. Several of the smaller Pyrex measuring cups or aluminum measuring cups will take care of the situation without a huge outlay of money. (Don't try to pinch pennies and use old orange juice cans or vegetable tins. Without a lip on your pouring container, you can't pour layers of wax. You can try, but you won't like the results.)

Even if you have not amassed any great amount of leftover wax, you can make layered candles. Heat a pound and a half or two pounds of medium-temperature paraffin in the top of a double boiler. Use a candy thermometer. When the wax reaches 180°, add stearine. When it reaches 200°, remove the double boiler from the heat, wipe the bottom of the melting pot dry with paper towels, and divide the melted wax by pouring it into two, three, or more small pouring containers. Add dyes to the liquid wax in the pouring containers, and test for color in the usual way (see page 18).

Keep the wax warm and molten by putting the pouring containers on trivets which have been placed in a pan of hot water. Almost everyone has a big, flat-bottomed roasting pan which can be used in this way. Bring the water in the pan to a boil, then turn the heat down so that the water just simmers. It isn't practical to clip a candy thermometer to the rim of each and every pouring container, but if you use trivets and keep the water in the pan just under the boiling point, the wax in the containers will remain liquid and it won't overheat.

If you're using leftover wax, you can disregard the double boiler. Put chunks of dyed wax into the pouring containers and place these on the trivets in the pan of hot water. The wax will melt. And if you own an electric fry pan, you won't even need trivets.

Electric pans have automatic temperature controls. Put the pouring containers into the pan, fill pan with water, set the temperature control at 200° and don't worry. The warm water surrounding the pouring containers will keep the wax at an even temperature, and with that automatic control nothing can get too hot.

Horizontal Stripes

When pouring wax in layers, do not tilt the mold and pour down the side as you would if you were pouring a one-color pillar candle. Pour carefully and directly into the bottom of the mold. Try not to splash wax on the wall of the mold.

Wicks and wick holders can get in the way of a good, clean pour, so pour into a wickless mold. If there is a hole in the bottom of the mold, seal it with masking tape or mold sealer.

After pouring the first layer of colored wax, let it set up and harden a bit. For a clear-cut line of separation between colors, the first layer of wax should be quite firm before the second layer is poured. For a gentler blending of color, the second layer can be poured while the first layer is still warm. Test the hardness of the first layer of wax by prodding it in the center with a pencil or the handle of a wooden spoon. The wax should be slightly tacky even if you want a sharp separation between your colored layers. It can be almost liquid if you want the colors to blend into one another.

A candle poured in layers will contract and sag in the middle just as surely as any other candle. Don't let this worry you. Save some wax when you pour the last layer. After the candle has set up and the depression appears in the center of this last layer, use your reserved wax to fill the depression and even off the top of the candle.

Water baths are not usually used for layered candles. Let the candle remain in the mold overnight, to make sure it is completely cold, then unmold it.

Wicking

Add a wick, using a hot ice pick to make a wick hole. A wire-core wick will insert most easily. The size depends on the size of the layered candle.

Diagonal Stripes

The easiest layered candle to make is one with regular horizontal stripes. A variation on this is the diagonally striped candle. You get diagonal stripes by tilting your mold.

Rest one side of the mold on a support. The support need not be any complicated gadget. It need only be stable. A

A variation on the layered candle is the one with diagonal stripes of color. The process is exactly the same as for layering, except that the mold is tilted as shown. The support for the mold can be very simple, but it must be stable.

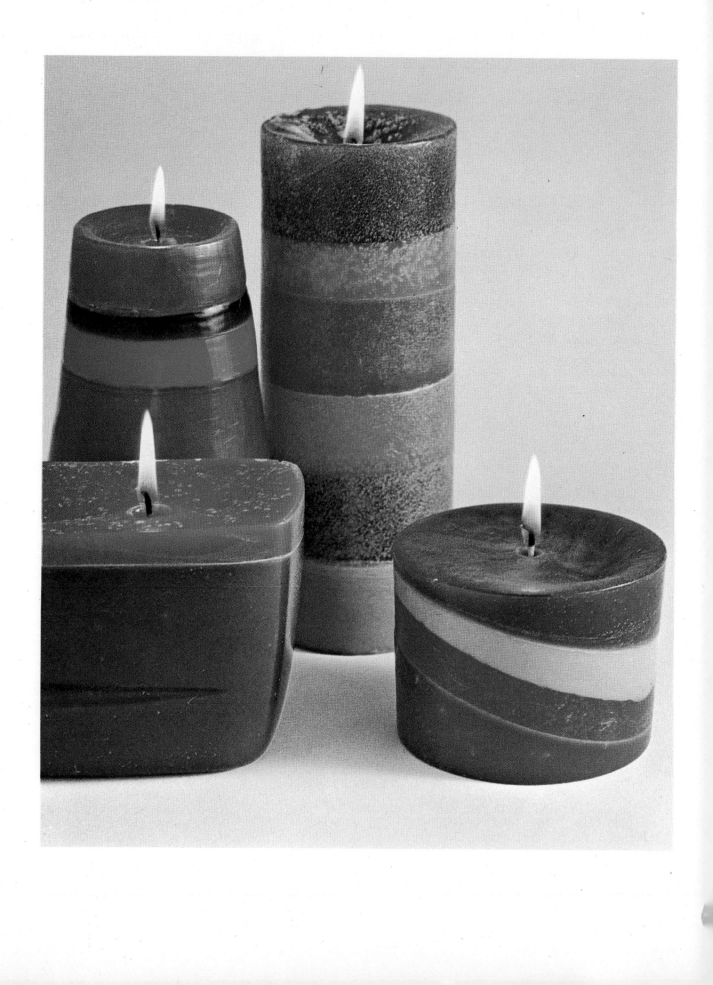

medium-thick paperback book or a little stack of magazines will do.

Pour a layer of color into the mold and let the wax set up. Then pour a second layer of color and let that set. If you're working with a third or fourth color, pour those layers. When the first three or four layers are firm, turn your mold and tilt it in the opposite direction, using the paperback book or the stack of magazines to keep it steady.

Pour several layers of color, letting each set up between pourings.

Tilt the mold again, if you wish.

When the layered wax has nearly reached the top of the mold, set the mold level. The last pouring should be all one color, and it must be poured when the mold is on the level. Reserve a little wax to fill any depression which may appear in the top of the candle.

The diagonally striped candle is unmolded and wicked just as the regular candle is unmolded and wicked. Make sure it has completely hardened before you remove it from the mold.

Mottling

If you want a mottled look in your layered candles, you can get it by adding oil to your melted wax just before pouring. No special mottling oil is needed. Almost any oil will mottle wax. Use a good quality oil, however—such as the fine machine oil used on sewing machines. Three teaspoons of oil to one pound of wax will be adequate.

Pouring

It is not wise to pour half of a layered candle one day and the second half another day. Once the layers of wax you poured on Day One cool and harden completely, they may not be receptive to the layers of wax you pour on Day Two. Cold wax is brittle, and it tries not to adhere to warm wax. If you start to pour wax in layers, finish in one grand operation—or you may have a candle which will do its best to break in half. You may also ruin the layered surface. Cold wax can pull away from the walls of the mold, and warm wax added to layers of cold wax can seep down between the cold wax and the mold and spoil the design of the candle. It can also bind the candle into the mold.

Stacked Candles

Cold wax tries not to adhere to warm wax. That is a fact of life and something a candlemaker needs to remember. Once the candlemaker knows the rules, he can often find ways to break them—or at least to work around them. The proof of this is the stack candle, which is molded in several parts and then put together with hot wax and wicking.

The most basic stack candle is the muffin-pan candle. All of the depressions in a muffin pan are the same size and the same shape. All are wider at the top than at the bottom. Wax rounds molded in a muffin pan will not vary more than a hair, one from another.

Begin construction of a stacked candle as you would begin any candle. Heat wax. Add stearine and dye. Remove wax from the heat.

Coat your mold—in this case, the muffin pan—with mold release.

Now pour. Fill each little cup in the muffin tin with hot wax.

Forget the water bath. Muffin pans are shallow and you might get water into the wax if you tried to put a muffin pan into a bath.

Let the wax in the muffin cups set up. The wax will shrink as it cools. Fill any depressions that appear so that all the muffin cups are level and full to the brim.

Wait until the wax muffins are solid and the muffin pan is cool to the touch. Then unmold the wax by turning the muffin pan upside down. The wax rounds should slide out easily, since muffin pans were made for easy unmolding.

Wicking

Calculate the exact center of your round wax muffins. This doesn't require an advanced degree in mathematics. Use a ruler and measure the width of the rounds. Halfway across is the center, and you can mark this by jabbing a pencil point into the wax.

With a hot ice pick, make a wick hole through the center of each round of wax.

A metal wick clip is a great help in wicking a stack candle. Select the wax round which will be the base of the candle. Use an electric pen or a soldering iron, if you have one, to make an indentation in the bottom of this round for the wick clip. If you don't have one of these, almost any implement which can be heated will do the job. You need only to melt

Muffin tins and ice trays make fine molds for sections of stacked candles. In fact, any container which will turn out a series of related waxen shapes can be used for stacks. Don't try to combine too many shapes; rounds put together with squares and triangles will not make a well-balanced, even-burning candle.

away a bit of the wax. Try a screwdriver or a can opener. (Don't use a paring knife; heating a knife blade can destroy the cutting edge.)

Insert the wick clip into the bottom of the wax round.

Cut a piece of wicking which will be several inches longer than the finished stacked candle. Knot one end of this wick. Thread the wick through the wick clip and the wick hole in the base of the candle. Pull the wick taut, so that the knot is right up against the wick clip.

Heat paraffin to 200°. Since cold wax does not want to stick to warm wax, make sure the wax which will fasten your stacked candle together is not just warm. It should be *hot*. Also, you may fare better if the pouring container for this hot wax has a spout rather than simply a pouring lip. The measuring cup will answer the purpose, but a small kettle with a spout will be neater, easier, and safer. Heat the wax right in the pouring container—over boiling water, of course— and use the candy thermometer.

Pour a little of the hot wax into the wick hole in the base of your candle.

Thread a second wax muffin onto the top of the wick. Do not immediately push this second round of wax down onto the round which will be the base of the candle. Wait for just a moment—long enough to pour a goodly dollop of that clear, hot paraffin on top of the base of the candle. (Watch your fingers; that's *hot* wax.) Then quickly slide the second wax round down the wick and press it against the first round in the stack. The hot wax will seal the two wax muffins together.

Pour a little hot wax into the wick hole of the second wax round.

Thread a third wax muffin onto the wick.

Pour hot wax on top of the second wax muffin and quickly slide the third round of wax into position on top of the second round.

Repeat this process, stacking one wax muffin atop another and sealing them into place with hot wax, until you have run through your supply of wax muffins or until your candle is as tall as you want it to be.

If any wax has dribbled or spurted out from between the sections of your stacked candle, it will have hardened by now and can be easily removed with a paring knife—or perhaps even with a fingernail.

Glazing

Holding the candle by the long wick, dip it into hot wax for a good glaze (see page 25), and also for added insurance that the stack will remain in one piece. Remember to allow for displacement when you dip the stack. The level of wax in your glazing container will rise as the candle is dipped.

Let the glaze harden, then trim off the extra wick.

Stacking

Stacked candles which are molded in muffin pans can be put together so that the wide part of each wax round is matched to the wide part of the next wax round, and the narrow parts of the rounds are matched to the narrow parts. There isn't any requirement that the stack be assembled this way. You can turn all the rounds one way. You can wick the stack so that it is a series of upside-down wax muffins. You can use all one color, or different colors. You can use a clear glaze or you can add dye to your glaze. You can do it any way you please.

In fact, you do not even need a muffin tin. All the elements in your stack of wax need not be the same size. Baking dishes come in graduated sizes and make beautiful molds for stacked candles.

At a certain point, common sense will set in. If you use molds of different sizes for a stacked candle, plan to use the largest wax round (or square, or whatever) as the base of the stack. The candle will be much more stable.

Also, do not try to combine shapes which have no relation to one another. Piling squares on top of rounds on top of ball shapes will not be very pleasing, and no matter how expertly you wick and seal the parts, you're apt to have a lopsided candle. Lopsided candles don't burn nicely. They fall over, and they sometimes break apart.

In assembling your stacked candle, use plenty of wick to allow for easier handling when you glaze. Make sure the wick hole is in the center of each wax round.

Chunk Candles

To make a chunk candle, you need all your regular candle-making supplies and you also need chunks of wax. The chunks should be colored, because colorless chunks are no fun at all. Beyond that, the approach to chunks depends on the temperament of the candlemaker.

If you have leftover wax, you may already have chunks. If you don't have leftover wax, you can make chunks.

Making Chunks

Heat medium-temperature paraffin in a melting pot or double boiler. Use a candy thermometer. When the wax reaches 180°, stir in stearine. Add dye and test for color.

Coat a flat-bottomed container with mold release. Candle-makers sometimes suggest using a cookie sheet for chunks, but cookie sheets are large. Unless you want heaps of chunks, a cake pan is satisfactory.

Pour the hot, dyed wax into the cake pan. How much you pour is up to you. How thick do you want your chunks to be? You can pour half an inch of wax, or three quarters of an inch, or more than an inch.

If you want free-form chunks, your task is simple. Let the wax in the pan get completely cold, then turn it out and break it up with a hammer.

If you want chunks that are more restrained—small squares or strips of wax—you will have to cut them. Don't let the wax in the pan get cold and hard. Let it solidify, but start cutting chunks while the wax is still warm and malleable. Use a paring knife to cut the warm wax, and work from the outer edge of the pan toward the center, since the wax in the center will not harden as quickly as the wax around the edges.

If you find that you have miscalculated, and the wax in the pan is too brittle to cut, you can start over. Re-melt the wax, pour it into the pan, and again wait for it to set up.

After you have cut all the wax in the pan into chunks, let the chunks get thoroughly hard, then turn the pan upside down. The chunks will drop out.

Once you have chunks, you can proceed to make a chunk candle.

With one or two exceptions, chunk candles are made exactly the way all molded candles are made. Prepare your work area and wick your mold in the usual manner.

Melt medium-temperature wax in a melting pot or double boiler, using a candy thermometer.

Chunks for your chunk candle can be as thick or as thin as your please. Cut them from a cake pan as the molten wax begins to harden, working from the outer edge of pan toward center. (The wax in the center remains liquid longest.)

Do not add stearine. Stearine makes wax opaque. You have gone to some trouble to achieve chunks, and you want them to show through the walls of your finished candle. So omit stearine.

If you use dye—and you probably will, since undyed wax looks gray—use it sparingly and choose a color that will complement your chunks—light yellow for orange chunks, or pale pink for hot pink chunks.

Pouring

When the wax in the melting pot is ready—that is, when dye has been added and the wax is at about 180°—put a handful of chunks into the mold. Pour liquid wax over these. Chunk candles are usually poured by inches, and one or two inches are as much as you should attempt on the first pour.

Omit the water bath. Let the wax set up around the chunks in the mold. Prod between the chunks with your ice pick and fill any air cavities that appear.

When the first pouring has set, add more chunks and more wax. Let the second pouring harden and fill air cavities.

Then add more chunks and more wax. Repeat until you have filled your mold or run out of chunks or liquid wax.

Let the candle remain in the mold overnight, then unmold and finish it as you would any other candle—trimming excess wax off the bottom with a cheese grater and rubbing the bottom on a hot griddle to smooth it. Cut off extra wick.

Variations

The chunk candle can be varied in several ways. For example, chunks made without stearine will melt more quickly than chunks containing stearine, and the candlemaker can use them for a marbled effect. He can put them in a mold and pour on very hot wax, so that the chunks blend and run together, coloring the candle from within. The smaller the chunks, the more easily they will melt and blend.

If you want to avoid marbling, add extra stearine to the wax you will use for chunks. When the chunks have set and are in the mold, don't cover them with very hot wax. Let the liquid wax cool to 170° or less.

If you are not satisfied with the showing your chunks make inside the finished candle, you can remove some of the wax from the surface of the candle by dipping the candle into hot water. Remember to allow for displacement. Use hot, but not boiling, water and be sure you have plenty of extra wick protruding from the candle. The best and safest way to dip a candle is to hold it by the wick.

Put wax chunks into wicked mold a handful at a time. An inch or two of chunks in the mold is enough to start. Then pour melted, dyed wax over chunks. When set, repeat.

Lace Candles

Wax and water will not mix, and because of this we have lace candles. The lace candle, which is also called the ice candle, consists of an inner candle or core candle surrounded by a shell of wax which has irregular holes in it. When the lace candle is lighted, the core candle will burn down into the wax shell, and the light will gleam out through the holes.

To make a lace candle, you should have a large-diameter mold. Your core candle can be an ordinary taper, bought at a store. It should not be taller than your mold, and when it is inserted into the center of the mold, there should be more than an inch of space between the core candle and the walls of the mold.

Wicking is no problem with a lace candle, since the core candle comes already wicked. You will get good results if you use a good metal mold, but seal the hole in the bottom of the mold with masking tape.

Melt medium-temperature wax in a double boiler or melting pot. Use a candy thermometer and add stearine and dye when the wax reaches 180°.

Pour about half an inch of liquid wax into the bottom of the mold. Set the bottom of the core candle in this wax and hold it steady, making sure it is in the center of the mold. The wax will harden around it and secure it.

Turn out a tray of ice cubes. Wrap the ice cubes in a towel and tap them with a hammer. Don't pulverize the ice. If each cube breaks into two or three pieces, your ice will do its part in making beautiful waxen lace.

For a lace candle, put cracked ice into a mold around the core candle. Start with about two inches of ice. Pour wax over ice until the ice is almost covered. When set, repeat.

Pouring

Drop this cracked ice into the mold until it surrounds the core candle to a depth of about three inches.

Pour melted wax over the cracked ice until the wax almost covers the ice.

Wait until this poured wax has hardened slightly, then add more cracked ice and more melted wax. Repeat, until the layers of ice and wax are level with the top of the core candle.

After the last pouring, you can hasten the cooling of the lace candle by putting the mold into a water bath for an hour or so. You do not need to test for well areas, since the core candle will not have any, and the outer wax shell is already full of holes.

Remove the mold from the water bath and let the candle cool at room temperature for six to eight hours.

Unmolding

It is a good idea to unmold a lace candle in the sink. Fold a dish towel to several thicknesses and put it in the sink. Tap the mold gently against this towel. The candle should slide out. All the ice will have turned to water, and this will run out of the candle.

Make sure that no pockets of water remain in the candle. Examine the lace shell carefully. If it appears that water has been trapped inside the wax, heat your trusty ice pick, make a small hole in the wax, and drain off the water.

Dry your mold carefully, and treat it with mold release to prevent rust.

There are purists who say that the core candle and the lace shell should be the same color. They certainly can be, but you can also experiment with contrasts. Try a red core candle and a white wax shell, or an orange candle with green lace, or any combination that appeals to you.

Burning

When a lace candle is lighted, there is always a possibility that molten wax from the burning core candle will run out through the holes in the lace shell. This can be very attractive, but use a large enough candle holder to allow for this. It is possible to remove wax stains from a tablecloth, but it's much easier simply to remove spilled wax from a candle holder.

Hurricane Candles

Hurricane candles aren't candles at all, since they have no wicks and they are not intended to be burned. A hurricane candle is a wax shell, and the best hurricane candles are cast in metal molds made especially for this purpose. They are large molds and they have no wick holes.

If you already have a good, big metal mold, you can make a hurricane candle in it. Close the wick hole in the bottom of the mold with masking tape.

It takes a large amount of wax to cast a hurricane candle. Figure on at least two quarts, or five and a half pounds. Prepare the wax as usual, melting it over boiling water and using a candy thermometer. When the wax reaches 200°, add dye. *Do not add stearine.* When the hurricane candle is finished, a votive light will be placed inside it. The glow from the votive light should shine through the wax hurricane shell, and so you want it to be translucent. Stearine would make it opaque.

Spray the hurricane mold with mold release and pour the melted wax into the mold to the desired height. Be sure to stop pouring when the wax is about an inch from the top of the mold.

Put the mold in a water bath and weigh it down if necessary.

Once the mold is in the water bath, watch it carefully. When the wax hardens across the top, start testing it with a knife. The walls of a hurricane candle will be about half an inch thick when the wax on the top of the candle is a quarter of an inch thick. That's the time to go into action.

With your paring knife, cut the hardened wax from the top of the candle. Insert the knife into the wax half an inch in from the wall of the mold and cut all the way around the mold, keeping the knife half an inch away from the wall. Then lift the layer of solid wax off the top of the candle.

Remove the mold from the water bath and dry the outside.

Pour the liquid wax from the mold into the melting pot.

What remains in the hurricane mold is a shell of wax about half an inch thick. This is your hurricane candle.

Allow it to cool for four or five hours inside the mold, then unmold it.

There may be some ragged spots on the top edge of the candle. These can be trimmed away with a knife, or they can be melted away by rubbing the edges of the candle gently on a hot griddle.

Put a votive candle inside the hurricane shell and light the votive candle. Then sit back and enjoy the glow.

A large-diameter candle and a small votive candle can be combined to simulate a hurricane candle. Let the wick in the large candle burn down an inch or two. Scoop out the molten wax. Repeat to depth desired. Put votive light into the resulting cavity. Its glow will shine through the walls of the larger candle.

Free-form candles are fun. Plastic sheeting was used to mold the candle on the right, and aluminum foil molded the candle below (see page 52 for directions). You can also make free-form candles in sand molds (see page 53).

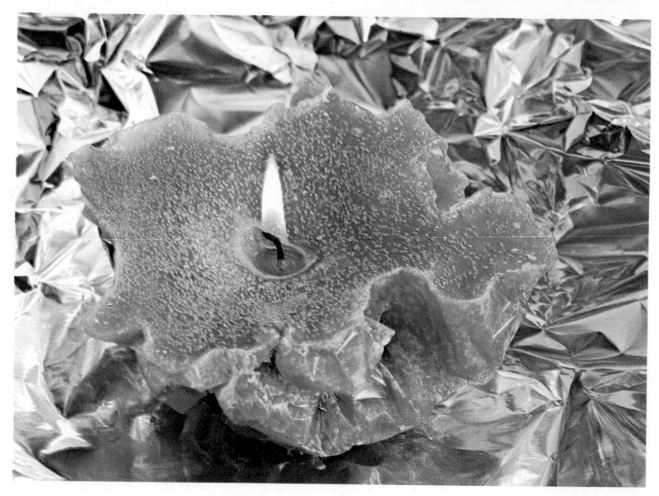

Free-form Candles

Almost anything with a cavity in it can be a candle mold, and for casting candles in odd and unusual shapes, some rather unusual material can be used.

There is plastic, for example. Plastic bowls and food containers are familiar to us, but there are also sheets of plastic. It covers the clothes that come from the cleaner. Most of us have rolls of it in our kitchen. We use it to wrap food.

At first glance, plastic wrap would seem to be about the most unlikely material on earth to use for a candle mold. It looks as if it would melt at about 10°F. It won't. It's tougher than that, and if a candlemaker exercises care, he can use it to fashion candles in some interesting shapes.

First, spray the plastic with mold release.

Next, make a cavity into which you can pour wax. This is simple. Push the plastic down into a glass jar. Let the edges hang out around the top of the jar. Slip a rubber band onto the top of the jar to hold the plastic in place.

Melt your wax in a double boiler or melting pot, adding stearine and dye when the wax reaches 180°. Remove wax from the heat. Let it cool until a scum forms on the surface.

Pouring

Carefully pour a little wax into the plastic cavity you have created inside the glass jar. If the wax melts through the plastic, you'll have to find another kind of plastic sheet. Chances are, however, that the wax won't melt through, and you can go ahead and fill the plastic sack with warm wax.

Allow the wax to cool for a short time. When it's no longer liquid, but still soft and pliable, remove the sack from the jar.

Close the top of the plastic container by bringing the ends together, giving them a slight twist and securing them with a piece of string or with the rubber band. Now you have a plastic bag filled with pliable wax. You can twist it, knead it, prod it, poke it, and mold it into any shape you want.

When you're satisfied with the shape of the wax, put the plastic sack into cool water and allow the wax to get hard.

Unmold your free-form candle by removing the string or rubber band and peeling the plastic away from the wax.

Wicking

Use a hot ice pick to make a wick hole in the mass of wax. Insert a wire-core wick (see page 15). If necessary, smooth the bottom by rubbing on a hot griddle.

When making a free-form candle in plastic sheeting, allow the wax to cool until it can be handled easily and safely, then remove it from its supporting jar to mold it into whatever shape you want.

Casting in Foil

Foil can be used for free-form candles in exactly the same manner as plastic. For wicking, use a hot ice pick and a wire-core wick. (See page 15.)

Aluminum foil is not nearly as malleable as plastic, but it is an excellent material for receiving hot wax. It is almost impossible to damage foil, and the candlemaker can pour into a foil container without fear of a wax break-through.

You can use foil as you would use plastic. Suspend a foil sack in a jar and fill it with hot wax. When the wax has cooled, but before it gets hard, remove the foil sack and shape the wax by hand. When the wax is solid, peel away the foil and wick the resulting free-form candle.

Be prepared for crinkles in the surface of the candle. Foil *will* crinkle. If you don't like the effect, remove it by dipping the candle into hot wax. (Make sure the wick is thoroughly set in the candle before you dip.)

Quieter adventures are possible when you mold with foil. You can fill a dishpan or an old pot with sand. Scoop out enough sand so that there will be a depression to receive the foil mold. Push the foil into that depression and fill the resulting foil mold with hot wax. The sand will support the mold until the wax sets up.

Foil-cast candles poured in layers are very popular. Interesting shapes can be achieved by creasing the foil before pouring the wax. After the candle is unmolded, the surface will be clean and glossy.

Wicking

It is easy to add a wick to a foil-cast candle after the candle is unmolded. But if you wish, you can wick a foil mold before you pour wax. Put a stick across the top of the mold and fasten a wire-core wick to this. Pull the wick straight and pour wax around it. As it cools, the wax will sag around the wick. Test for well areas and add hot wax to fill in the sagging depression.

Sand-cast Candles

There are almost no limits to what an imaginative candlemaker can do with sand and wax. Sand-cast candles can be deep or shallow, layered, mottled, decorated, plain, glazed or unglazed, carefully shaped or delightfully free.

For sand-casting, you will need all the candle equipment you have (except molds), and you will also need sand. Nice, clean sand is what is required—sand free of small sticks and bits of leaves and other unsightly stuff. Go to the nearest builders' supply company and look over the stock. Select what appeals to you and bring the sand home.

Prepare your wax in the usual way—melting, adding stearine and dye, watching your candy thermometer.

Preparing the Mold

While the wax is melting, prepare your sand mold. Put your sand into a container and add water. The sand must be damp, or it will not hold any shape at all. It shouldn't be so wet that it's runny, but it must be thoroughly damp all the way through.

Make a cavity in the damp sand. If you want a free-form candle, you will use your hands to make the cavity. If you're feeling more formal, press some object into the sand so that the cavity will have a definite shape. A bowl or a vase can be used to shape sand. (Naturally, you will remove the object from the sand before you pour wax.)

When the hole in the sand is pleasing to you, and the wax is ready, fill the hole with liquid wax.

As the candle sets up, fill any sags and wells that appear.

Let the candle remain in the sand mold overnight.

Unmold the candle by removing the wax from the sand. Since sand can be messy, do the unmolding outside.

Make a wick hole with a hot ice pick and insert a wire-core wick—and there's your sand candle!

Variations

There are endless, delightful variations on this basic process, and you will probably think of more as you work with sand and wax.

You may want a candle with a thick crust of sand. If you do, pour wax into the sand mold at 200°.

If you don't want a very thick crust on your sand-cast candle, pour cooler wax—at about 150°.

If you want a free-form candle with almost no sand on it, take the candle out of doors and turn a hose on it. Some of the sand will wash away. What remains can be removed. Either dip the candle into hot water (making sure that the wick is firmly embedded in the wax, and allowing for displacement) or get a propane torch. Small propane torches are not expensive, and they are marvelous for glazing large candles, for removing unwanted patches of sand, and for softening and sculpturing free-form candles.

One wick is adequate for a sand-cast candle, but more than one can be inserted into the candle if the candle is large.

You can fashion a candle for which sand is a container. Mix melted wax with dry sand. Add enough wax so that the mixture is like dough, and work quickly before the wax can harden.

Spray mold release into a bowl or a foil mold.

Line the bowl or the mold with the combination of wax and sand, pressing the mixture against the mold with your fingers.

Allow the wax and sand mixture in the mold to harden.

Pour colored, scented wax into this sand mold.

After the resulting candle has hardened, remove it from the bowl or the mold. Use your ice pick (heated) to make a wick hole and insert a wire-core wick.

Sand for the sand-cast candle must be thoroughly damp all the way through. If you are making a free-form candle, you can use your hands to make a cavity in the sand (left). After wax has hardened, unmold your sand-cast candle by removing it from the sand.

Flower Candles

Candles with flowers embedded in them are somewhat like lace candles in that they are made in two parts. There is a center candle—a core candle—and an outer shell of wax which contains the floral decorations.

To make a flower candle, you need all the usual candle-making supplies, a core candle, a fairly large-diameter mold, and some flowers and leaves.

If you wish, make the core candle yourself. The size is up to you, but the core candle must be about an inch less in diameter than the mold for the flower candle. It is perfectly legitimate to buy a pillar candle and use it for the core candle, but keep in mind the relative size of the mold and the core candle. You will need that inch of room.

Pin flowers and leaves to the core candle.

Wicking

Insert the core candle into the mold, wick first. Thread the wick through the wick hole in the bottom of the mold and secure it by sealing the hole with masking tape.

If you are using a pillar candle which you have purchased for the core candle, threading that bit of wick through a wick hole may be a challenge. Help yourself along by tying a string to the wick, threading that through the hole and drawing the core candle after it.

If you are using a candle which you yourself have made for a core candle, leave lots of extra wick on top of the candle and thread this through the wick hole in the bottom of the mold. Then insert the core candle with the flowers pinned to it, draw the wick tight at the bottom of the mold and secure it with masking tape.

Melt paraffin and add dye that will blend with the color of your inner core candle. Don't add stearine; you want the outer wax shell of the candle to be translucent so that the flowers will show through.

Pouring

Pour wax into the space between the core candle and the wall of the mold. Pouring temperature should be about 180°. You can use a water bath if you wish, but it isn't really necessary. Watch the wax set up, prod around the core candle with your ice pick and fill any well areas that appear.

When the flower candle is cold—after several hours—unmold it as you would any candle.

For a flower candle, you need a core candle, a large-diameter mold, plastic flowers and leaves, and pins for fastening flowers to the candle.

After pinning flowers and leaves to the core candle, put the candle into your mold and pour warm wax into the space between mold and candle.

Be sparing with dyes when making a flower candle. Pale colors like pink, yellow, light blue, and white are best, since they will not compete too strongly with the color of the flowers.

Plastic flowers are also best, since real flowers may wilt when exposed to hot wax. You need not confine yourself to plastic flowers, however. Experiment. Try dried leaves, bits of pine branch, or any piece of greenery that appeals to you.

If you want your flower candle to have an "exfoliated" look—that is, if you want the surface of the flowers to extend beyond the surface of the candle—melt away some of the wax shell surrounding the core candle by rolling the candle in hot water—hot, not boiling.

For an exfoliated candle, it is possible to avoid the two-step process. Pin flowers to the surface of a pillar candle, then dip the candle into a glaze of warm wax. Remember to allow for displacement, and don't worry about the pins. They won't show through the wax, and part of the fun of candlemaking is finding ways to cheat.

For best results, make sure that the plastic flowers in your flower candle touch the walls of the mold so they will show through the outer wax shell. Use a pastel color for the wax shell, and don't use any stearine.

Ball Candles

In November, when the Christmas decorations go up in the department stores, the urge to make round candles often sweeps over candlemakers. A wax snowball with a wick in it is a charming Christmas gift, and it doesn't cost all outdoors.

To make a ball candle, you need a round mold. Ordinary household containers like mixing bowls have a way of not being truly round. Check your cupboards; if you find a bowl or cup with a round bottom, you are in business. If you don't —and you probably won't—you can still be in business. There are a number of approaches to ball candles. Choose the one that suits you.

Two-part Molds

You can visit the hobby shop and buy a round mold. These are two-part molds. There are metal molds and plastic molds for ball candles, and the molds come complete with instructions as to assembling, wicking, and pouring temperatures. (If the mold is metal, the pouring temperature will be the same as for any metal mold—that is, about 180°–200°.)

Prepare the wax as you would for any candle. Pour the melted wax into the wicked mold. Let it begin to set up, then break the surface tension with your ice pick and fill any well areas, just as you would if you were pouring a pillar candle. When the candle has cooled completely, unmold it by opening the two-part mold. Remove any seam line with a paring knife and, if necessary, flatten the bottom of the ball candle by rubbing it on a hot griddle.

Making Your Own Plaster-of-Paris Mold

If you decide not to invest in a two-part ball mold, you can still pour round candles. Make your own half-round molds using plaster of Paris. Get a ball that is the size you want your candle to be. A visit to a toy shop or a variety store will take care of that. The best ball for this purpose is one with a seam running around the center. It saves all sorts of trouble; you don't have to figure out exactly how much ball is half a round.

The plaster of Paris comes from the hobby shop with instructions for mixing and pouring.

Prepare the plaster of Paris and pour it into a container. Let it set slightly and then put the ball into it. Press down until the plaster covers exactly half the ball. Let the plaster of Paris harden, then remove the ball.

Now get another container, prepare another batch of plaster

Two half-round molds can be used for a ball candle. Shape the molds by pressing a ball into containers of plaster of Paris. After molding two half-rounds of wax, cut a groove across one, lay the wick into the groove, then fasten the halves together with very hot wax—200°.

of Paris, let it set slightly, and then press the ball into it until half the ball is covered. After the plaster has hardened, remove the ball.

You now have two half-round molds. After they have dried completely, coat the cavities with mold release and fill them with hot wax. As the wax cools and settles, be sure to fill the centers with melted wax so that the finished halves of the ball will fit together perfectly.

Wicking

When the wax is hard, turn it out of the molds. With a knife, make a groove along the center of the flat surface of one half ball. Lay a wick in this groove and pour very hot wax—200° wax—over the flat surface and the wick. Then quickly press the second half ball of wax onto the first to form a complete ball of wax.

Let the candle harden completely so that the two halves are firmly joined and the wick is solidly set in the candle. Smooth away any seam line with a paring knife and trim off extra wick. Flatten the bottom of the candle by rubbing it on a hot griddle.

Disposable Glass Molds

In addition to two-part metal or plastic molds and do-it-yourself plaster-of-Paris molds, there are glass breakaway molds available for ball candles. These are round glass vials with narrow necks for receiving melted wax. They must be destroyed as the candle is unmolded, but they are not expensive and are easy to use for small ball candles. Be sure to warm them slightly (see page 32), and set them in a container of sand to hold them upright. Pour in wax at about 170°, watch the wax set up, and break the surface tension so that you can fill any well areas that appear. When the wax is cold, unmold the ball candle by breaking the glass gently. Trim away any excess wax that may have collected around the area of the pouring spout with a knife. Make a wick hole with a hot ice pick and add a wire-core wick to the candle.

One of the nicest snowball candles is a red candle frosted with white whipped wax. If you want an all-white candle, or a blue one, or even a lavender one, that's up to you, but the red snowball with white frosting is the odds-on favorite.

Whipped Wax

Make wax frosting by whipping warm wax just as you'd whip cream. Melt the wax in the top of the double boiler and add a goodly amount of stearine so it will be nice and white. Let

After the two halves of this ball candle were put together, it was dipped in bright red wax.

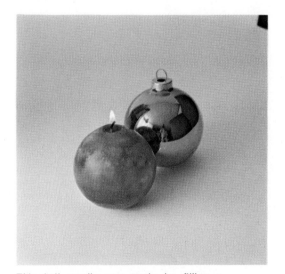

This ball candle was made by filling a Christmas ornament with wax, then breaking the ornament after the wax hardened.

the wax cool until scum forms on the top. With an electric mixer or a rotary egg beater, whip this scum until it becomes a lather. Then spoon it out and frost the snowball with it exactly the way you would frost a cake.

Don't try to whip an entire pot of wax at one time. Beat the top layer of scum and use that. Work quickly, so that the whipped wax doesn't harden before you can get it onto the candle. While you are frosting the snowball, a second layer of scum will be forming on the melted wax. Whip that after you have used up the lather from the first layer. You can whip a third batch and a fourth batch and a fifth if you need to, and if the wax in the double boiler gets too solid for whipping, you can put it back on the heat and melt it again.

Clean the egg beater or the blades of the electric mixer by putting them on foil in a warm oven to melt off the wax. Then wash them in hot water and soap.

One classic way to use whipped wax is to frost a ball candle and make a Christmas snowball. Another is to fill a sundae glass for a parfait candle. Parfait candles can be all whipped wax (strawberry is a nice color) or part plain wax, as here. A white whipped-wax topping looks like whipped cream. The beer-stein candle on page 32 is a variation on this, except that the power of suggestion turns the wax to white foam.

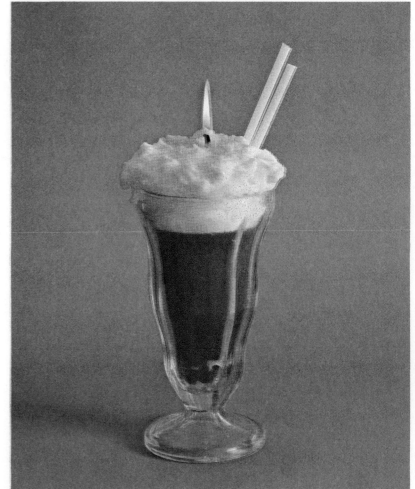

Candles in Containers

Not all candles are meant to be unmolded. Parfait candles like the one on the facing page and beer-stein candles (see page 32) remain in their sundae glasses and steins, and any nice container—from a pickle jar to a flowerpot to a covered candy dish—can be a candle holder if *you* decide that it is. Fill it with wax and wick, and light it.

There are only a few special things to remember when making candles that are to be burned in the containers in which they are molded:

Use a lower temperature wax so that the candle will burn evenly all the way across and will use itself up entirely as it burns.

If you value the container, don't try to insert the wick after you have poured the wax. Pre-wick the candle using the method pictured on page 31.

If you are using a clear glass container, use a dyed wax. For a colored glass container, a clear or very lightly colored wax will work best. If your container is opaque, like the flowerpot shown here, use the colors that suit you—and the container.

After burning the candle, you can clean the container as you would any candlemaking utensil. Put it into a warm oven and let the leftover wax melt off onto a sheet of foil.

Glassware, cheese crocks, flowerpots, openwork bricks or cement blocks (see the example on page 2)—any of these can be used as attractive and unusual candle holders.

Decorating Candles

There is almost no end to the things that can be done with wax to make candles more personal, more decorative, and more special. For example:

Pour a very thin layer of red wax onto a pie plate. With a tiny cookie cutter, cut out tiny hearts as the wax begins to harden. Press the hearts to a white pillar candle while they are still soft, and fuse the edges against the candle with a hot ice pick. (The same general procedure—using different shapes and different colors—was used to decorate the appliqué candle at top left of the facing page.)

Dip a white taper into intensely dyed liquid wax. Let the layer of dyed wax harden for a few minutes and then dip the taper again. Punch polka dots out of the still-soft layer of dyed wax with the blunt end of a pencil (eraser removed).

Apply photographs, prints, lettering, or any paper pattern to a candle. Heat clear wax, then dip the paper into the wax with tweezers. Apply it quickly to the candle. When it is set in place, dip the entire candle for a smooth finish.

Pin flowers and leaves or paper lace to the outside of a candle. Sequins, fake jewels, seed pearls, and cotton lace also make good pin-on decorations.

Paint your own design on a plain candle. The hobby shops offer paints manufactured especially for use on candles. These can be applied with a camel's hair brush, and they dry instantly. Painted candles can be finished by dipping them into a clear glaze.

Dribble brightly colored wax over a pastel candle. There are waxes especially made for this purpose. Called "dribble waxes," they are softer and more adhesive than regular paraffin, and some fluorescent colors are available. You can dribble wax over the top of the candle, letting it run down the sides, or you can place the candle on its side and dribble so that the colored wax encircles the candle (see the examples on page 5).

Whip a batch of wax (see pages 59–60) and use it to fasten a three-dimensional ornament to a candle. Lay the candle on its side, apply a blob of whipped wax, then embed the ornament in the wax. Let the entire thing harden before standing the candle erect, or the whipped wax may run down the side of the candle.

These ideas are only beginnings. From here on, you're on your own. Use your imagination. Let yourself go. Have fun!

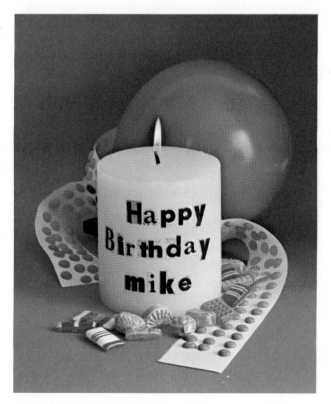

These are just a few of the many creative possibilities for decorating the outside of candles. Directions (and more ideas) will be found on the facing page. But be sure to experiment on your own—it's half the fun!

Suppliers

GENERAL SUPPLIES

WAX, WICKING, MOLDS, STEARINE, DYES, SCENTS

Ajello Candles
484 State Highway No. 17
Paramus, New Jersey 07652

Park Avenue and 50th Street
New York, New York 10022

The Candle Shop
111 Christopher Street
New York, New York 10014
(no mail order)

CCM Arts and Crafts, Inc.
9520 Baltimore Avenue
College Park, Maryland 20740
(mail order only)

Earth Wax Candles
24 East 21st Street
New York, New York 10010
(no mail order)
(visitors welcome to watch
candlemaking)

Economy Crafts
47–11 Francis Lewis Boulevard
Flushing, New York 11361

The Glow Candle Company
4052 Main Street
Kansas City, Missouri 64111

Box 10102
Kansas City, Missouri 64111
(mail order address)

LeeWards
512 South U.S. Highway No. 19
Bellas Hess Store
Clearwater, Florida 33516

840 North State Street
Elgin, Illinois 60120

925 East 162nd Street
South Holland, Illinois 60473

10400 West 63rd Street
Shawnee, Kansas 66203

Schoenherr Road at 13-Mile Road
Warren, Michigan 56762

7737 Nicollet Avenue
Richfield, Minnesota 55423

110 Wilson Road
Great Western Shopping Center
Columbus, Ohio 43204

6851 Southland Drive
Middleburg Heights, Ohio 43336

300 Plymouth Park Shopping Center
Irving, Texas 75060

Elgin, Illinois 60120
(mail order address)

The Village Barn
Route 4, Box 159
Williamsburg, Virginia 23185

SPECIAL WAXES

BAYBERRY WAX

Ajello Candles
484 State Highway No. 17
Paramus, New Jersey 07652

Park Avenue and 50th Street
New York, New York 10022

BEESWAX

Ajello Candles
484 State Highway No. 17
Paramus, New Jersey 97652

Park Avenue and 50th Street
New York, New York 10022

The Candle Shop
111 Christopher Street
New York, New York 10014
(no mail order)

CCM Arts and Crafts, Inc.
9520 Baltimore Avenue
College Park, Maryland 20740
(mail order only)

Economy Crafts
47–11 Francis Lewis Boulevard
Flushing, New York 11361

The Glow Candle Company
4052 Main Street
Kansas City, Missouri 64111

Box 10102
Kansas City, Missouri 64111
(mail order address)